How to

Receive

Pastors'

Blessings

Spencer Dafe Itive

How to Receive Pastors' Blessings

Published By Chiysonovelty International, 2016

chiyson@minister.com

Tel: +2348027647777, +2348035922004

ISBN: 9785033708
ISBN-13: 978-9785033700

Printed in the United States of America

To God Be the Glory, Great Things He has done.

DEDICATION

This book is dedicated to all Born Again Christians, who have genuine love in their hearts, and are ready to serve God faithfully and willingly.

"Nature is not always lenient, if you break any law of nature, you pay for it." - Spencer Dafe Itive

CONTENTS

Dedication   IV

Acknowledgments   VII

Introduction   1

1   Chapter One   Pg #4

    Protocols & Etiquette

2   Chapter Two   Pg #10

    Understanding Authority

3   Chapter Three   Pg #20

    The Concept of Spiritual Authority

4   Chapter Four   Pg #39

    The Concept of the Prophet's Reward

5   Chapter Five   Pg #54

    The Dynamics of Giving

6   Chapter Six   Pg #77

    The Obligation of Praying for Pastors

7   Chapter Seven   Pg #87

    General Obligations to Pastors

8   Chapter Eight   Pg #98

    Roles and Responsibilities of Pastors to Members

9   Chapter Nine   Pg #109

    Gift of Peace

    About the Book   Pg #122

    About the Author   Pg #123

ACKNOWLEDGMENTS

I want to first and foremost acknowledge the blessed Holy Spirit for guiding and teaching me the truth concerning successful and gainful Christian service, especially how to be a son of consolation to my pastor. To him be glory, honour and majesty forever, Amen.

To Revd. Chris Okhiulu & Pst (*Mrs.*) Queen Okhiulu of Goodnews Mission Int'l Inc.: My Spiritual parents, thank you for exposing me to gainful God's service, your constant teachings have made me become better by the day.

Finally, to my one and only ever beautiful, young and beloved Angel, Mrs. Agatha Spencer: your love, care, prayers, encouragement, and support enrich every area of our lives together. And to my beloved children: God's Covenant, Rhema, and Amen; for the joy you brought; Daddy and Mummy love you so dearly.

Spencer Dafe Itive

INTRODUCTION

"And if a man also strive for masteries, yet is he not crowned, Except he strive lawfully." **2 Timothy 2:5**

Anything you are doing in this life has a better way of doing it! There are principles behind every operation in life. Simply put, life has rules!

Being skillful and talented is not always enough. One needs to discover, understand and deliberately obey certain life principles to be able to soar higher. God's services are no exceptions. One can only enjoy life in God's service if one strives for it lawfully.

The journey to unlimited blessings in God's vineyard begins with learning, learning, and more learning. However, ignorance characterizes the journey to a life of struggle and pain in God's vineyard. The right to make a choice between knowledge and ignorance is absolutely yours.

1

Apostle Paul writing to Timothy on this matter said:

"... that thou mayest know how thou oughtest to behave Thyself in the house of God ..." **1 Timothy 3:15**

There are countless blessings in serving God. How to get these blessings should be vital to anyone that desires these blessings. The secret to a world of uninterrupted gains lies in your pastor – God's servant over your life.

The pastor set over you can be for your rising or for your falling. He's the key to your world of unlimited blessings.

This book will help you gain the right orientation about your pastor and the authority he wields which you may have either under-utilized or undermined.

As you read through it with an open mind, light will come your way and deliver substance into your hand and life. So do well to reflect on these basic truths.

"Anyone who welcomes a prophet, just because that person is a prophet, will be given the same reward as a prophet..." **Mathew 10:41 (*CEV*)**

... You can enjoy the pastor's reward.

CHAPTER ONE

PROTOCOLS & ETIQUETTE

"And if man also strive for masteries, yet is he not crowned, Except he strive lawfully."

2 Timothy 2:5

"…Through knowledge shall the just be delivered."

Proverbs 11:9

CHAPTER # 1

PROTOCOL AND ETIQUETTE

"...You will know how everyone who belongs to God's family ought to behave... "

1 Timothy 3:15 (*CEV*)

"No one wins athletic contest without obeying the rules."

2 Timothy 2:5 (*CEV*)

The protocol is rules of etiquette and diplomacy; it is the right way to do things. There are right and wrong ways of doing things even in the Church of God. As believers, we're called out from a life of mediocrity into a life of excellence. We have to discover for ourselves via the word of God and the help of the Holy Spirit the right and acceptable way to function in God's Vineyard. If this doesn't happen, we live our lives with little or no meaningful progress.

Etiquette, which usually goes hand in hand with ethics "reflects who a person is." It is the customary rules for conduct or behavior in polite or ideal society. We all know the Church to be an ideal place. Christians' ethics differ from secular ethics because of it's link to the Bible and it's bases on the unchanging truth of scriptures.

There are rules for appropriate behavior and conduct for every environment. How such environment becomes accessible to you is a function of how well you understood the protocol for accessibility.

Protocol and etiquette will take you higher in life than ability and intelligence would, therefore be acquainted with protocol and etiquette.

The following keys are important in the teachings found in this book:

#1: Protocol grants you easy and quick access to the throne of God:

"Enter into his gates with thanksgiving and into his court with praise."

Psalm 100:4

`I have heard Christians say, we are going to bombard heaven's gates with prayers tonight`. They usually say this when they feel that God did not respond on time to their requests.

However, I ask: `Why will you bombard his throne with prayers when a simple act of praise and worship soaked in thanksgiving will open any door for you? ` It's only terrorists that bombard places and I don't believe you are terrorists.

#2: You need the protocol to thrive in your place of destiny.

"And David behaved himself wisely in all his ways; and the Lord was with him."

1 Samuel 18:14

No environment abhors good behaviour. In other words, good behaviours thrive everywhere. A wise child understands that no two environments are the same, in the same vein, no two pastors or churches are the same.

#3. Understand the Protocol to Connect to your Pastor

"… believe his prophets, so shall ye prosper."

2 Chronicles 20:20

"He that receiveth a prophet in the name of a prophet shall receive a prophet's reward…"

Mathew 10:41

The protocol is a vital instrument when it comes to relating with one's pastors. The God's servant over your life is honourable so treat him as such. He's a vital channel via which your blessings and miracles are triggered off.

Many of God's blessings to us come via the pastors

set over us. He is the intermediary between the Church members and God. You can hardly prosper outside him.

As long as one's a member of a particular Church, he or she can hardly prosper outside the pastor set over him or her in that local assembly.

Adequate study and revelations on the protocols involved in relating with one's pastor is essential. Journey with us as we unveil the truths one after the other in this timely masterpiece. Yes, you will learn how one can relate with his or her man of God effectively.

Don't be like the class of people described in this verse below, humble yourself and be tutored by the Holy Spirit

"...*people who think they know so much don't know anything at all.*"

1 Corinthians 8:2 (*CEV*)

CHAPTER TWO

UNDERSTANDING AUTHORITY

"… I sent Moses, Aaron and Miriam to be your leaders."

Micah 6:4 (*CEV*)

CHAPTER #2

UNDERSTANDING AUTHORITY

"Christ chose some of us to be apostles, prophets, missionaries, pastors, teachers; so that his people would learn to serve and his body would grow strong."

Ephesians 4:11-12 (CEV)

Authority is real, and God ordains it. God is a God of Authority. Each day we submit to one form of authority or the other. The kingdom of God is well-structured, same goes for the Church. Life itself is structured; hence, it is ruled by principles. Everything in life is ordained by God including authority.

The concept of authority must be well understood and obeyed for everyone to get the best out of life. Life answers to principles and protocols, that's because life is meant to be hierarchical and

11

coordinated. Any level of life you find yourself in came because of the choice or choices you've made in life.

Authority can be classified in the following ways:

#1 Professional Authority

#2 Marital Authority

#3 Parental Authority

#4 Civil/Government Authority

#5 Spiritual Authority

#1: Professional or Sapiential Authority:

One possesses this authority on grounds of knowledge and special training .A person who is more knowledgeable about a subject than others is said to be an authority on that subject.

"I know that you have workers who are experts at cutting lumber in Lebanon …"

2 Chronicles 2:18 (*CEV*)

"... *We both know that your workers are more experienced than anyone else at cutting lumber.*"

1 King 5:6 (*CEV*)

"...*They read a lot of books and became well educated...*"

Daniel 1:7 (*CEV*)

#2: Marital Authority

This particular authority exists between husband and wife. By virtue of marriage, the husband becomes an authority over his wife. While both of them are to submit to each other, the woman must realize that her husband is automatically her head and the head of the family, as Christ is the Head of the Church. Queen Vashti defaulted in this area and lost her crown as well as throne to young Queen Esther.

"*For the husband is the head of the wife, even as Christ is the head of the Church; and he is the Saviour of the body. Therefore as the church is subject unto Christ, so let the WIVES be to their own husbands in everything"*

Ephesians 5:23-14

#3: Parental Authority

This is both biological and spiritual. Your parents are in charge of your prosperity – both natural, spiritual etc. Your biological parent is a picture of where you are coming from while your Spiritual parent is a picture of where you are going to.

The imperfection of your parents does not permit your disloyalty.

"Children, obey your parents in the Lord: for this is right."

Ephesians 6:1

"Honour thy father and thy mother: that thy days may be long upon the land which the Lord thy God giveth thee."

Exodus 20:12

#4: Civil / Governmental Authority

God-ordained authority including civil and government; government or civil officials are therefore accountable to God regarding their actions – abuse and misuse of such authority.

"Obey the rulers who have authority over you. Only God can give authority to anyone, and he puts these rulers in their places of power. People who oppose these authorities are opposing what God has done, and they will be punished."

Romans 13:1-2 (CEV)

God has not only established authority among men, He also honours their judgment and punishment. The law- breakers are usually those who have issues with the law. In the same vein, those who don't like authority will have issues submitting to authority even in the Church. The ones who understand the principle of authority will as well understand and honour the principle of submission.

The verses below explain it better:

"You must also pay your taxes. The authorities are God's servants, and it is their duty to take care of these matters. Pay all that you owe, whether it is taxes and fees or respect and honour."

Romans 13:6-7 (*CEV*)

"Remind your people to obey the rulers and authorities and not to be rebellious. They must always be ready to do something helpful and not say cruel things or argue. They should be gentle and kind to everyone."

Titus 3:1-2 (*CEV*)

#5. Spiritual Authority

The world does not have the right protocol and knowledge of God's way of doing things; even, most believers do not either. Unlike the world that operates democracy, God's kingdom operates theocracy. The king has specific guidelines on how his kingdom is to governed. The institution of Spiritual authority and leadership in the body of Christ is ONE of such guidelines.

Spiritual Authority is God's established offices or positions of authority within the places of worship. It is a kind of delegated authority.

"Every high priest is appointed to help others by offering gifts and sacrifices to God because of their sins. But no one can have the honour of being a high priest simply by wanting to be one, only God can choose a priest, and God is the one who chooses Aaron."

Hebrews 5:1 & 4 (*CEV*)

"...And he gave some, apostles; and some, prophets; and some, evangelists; and some, Pastors and teachers."

Ephesians 4:11

Jesus is the head of the Church; He established these offices as well as ordained leaders with authority in these offices for the Church. God gave these leaders the responsibility to serve, oversee and establish His word and commands for His Church on the earth.

This Authority God sent over you is the channel via which your blessings come through as you faithfully serve in your local Assembly. Without mincing words, spiritual authority is the most important of all the types of authorities discussed in this book.

It should be noted that the God's Servant who is the head in any Church possesses the highest authority; other ministers or office holders should submit to him. His age is immaterial in this regard. He is the link between God, the church members and their blessings.

It is important members don't allow his humanity, flaws, age, idiosyncrasies, lack of education etc, rub them of their inherent blessing in God's service.

The Pastor is God's Servant over the life of his members, he possess enormous powers and influence than they may know. How well they relate with Him through appropriate protocol will open their channel of blessing and deliver results to them.

"If you do everything that your father did the way he did it, you can never be greater than your father."

Anonymous

CHAPTER THREE

THE CONCEPT OF SPIRITUAL AUTHORITY

"My friends, we ask you to be thoughtful of your leaders who work hard and tell you how to live for the Lord...."

1 Thessalonians 5:12 (*CEV*)

CHAPTER # 3

THE CONCEPT OF SPIRITUAL AUTHORITY

"Ten thousand people may teach you about Christ, but I am your only father ..."

1 Corinthians 4:15 (*CEV*)

What is Spiritual Authority?

This is God-ordained offices and positions of authority within a local Church- the body of Christ. It is the authority delegated by God to Pastors and others called to lead in local Assemblies.

Pastors or Heads of churches receive authority from God to ensure divinely inspired direction for the church. They preach and teach God's word, correct false teaching, and help believers in such churches to live a healthy Christian life.

God has assigned every believer to a particular church under the leadership of a pastor. You are to

21

submit to his spiritual leadership as a way of connecting to him. When it comes to relating to spiritual authority, it is crucial to learn an appropriate conduct and protocol per time.

Christians must learn how to properly and effectively relate to their spiritual heads so that they do not short-circuit God's plans for their lives when they by- pass their Pastors.

The purpose of this generational book, a life-saving balm, is to teach you the important role of your pastor in your life and your obligations to him. This will enable you get the best of him and so fulfill your divine purpose.

To understand this well, we shall be considering some fundamental but neglected protocols towards our spiritual leaders.

#1. The Protocol of Submission:

"Obey them that have the rule over you, and submit

yourselves: for they watch for your souls, as they that must give account, that they may do it with joy, and not with grief: for that is unprofitable for you."

Hebrews 13:7

"Submit yourselves to every ordinance of man for the Lord's sake ..."

1 Peter 2:13

"Likewise, you younger people, SUBMIT yourselves to your ELDERS..."

1 Peter 5:5

"People who oppose the authorities are opposing what God has done, and they will be punished."

Romans 13:2 (*CEV*)

Believers have an obligation to submit to the authority of those whom God ordained to serve as their leaders. Rebellion against God's established authorities is rebellion against God; no sane believer should try it.

True submission is an attitude of the heart. It speaks of respect, love, giving and humility. Only those who have yielded completely to God can fully understand it. It requires grace to submit unreservedly to a man that is imperfect. Submission is the most essential of all your obligations to spiritual leadership.

Submission is practical; it's something you practice per time until it becomes part of you. A submissive believer shows respect for those in authority, bearing in mind that their roles and calling is from God.

Blessing and anointing will not flow from the grace you neither submit to nor recognize. Submission is full-time and not part- time.

Submission to pastors is a relationship of love, honour to God, and then man. It is a principle that every believer should practice. It is a godly injunction, a divine principle for SAFETY and

SUCCESS. *Understand the principle of submission and the practice of submission will be easier.*

Authority flows from a higher to a lower person. Your pastor wields enormous power and influence spiritually because he's under authority too. *You have to submit to authority to be an authority.*

"Ye are they which have continued with me in my temptations and I appoint unto you a kingdom, as my father hath appointed unto me; that ye may eat and drink at my table in my kingdom, and sit on THRONES judging the twelve tribes of Israel."

Luke 22:28-30

"So I will give you the right to rule as kings, just as my father has given me the right to rule as a king."

Luke 22:29 (CEV)

Obviously, if you're not under anyone's authority, nobody will be under yours. The fact that you are under someone's authority is enough reason for others to be under your authority. Every successful leader must have a leader whom he submits to. In the same vein, every Pastor must submit to another Pastor with higher authority. With this, he can function effectively; otherwise, he'll be a tyrant. There is no calling that is higher than authority. *Be more sensitive to the anointing in a man's life than his feeling for you.*

#2. The Protocol of Loyalty

"...do all that is in thine heart: turn thee; behold, I am with thee according to thy heart."

1 Samuel 14:7

"...do what you think best, I'm with you all the way."

1 Samuel 14:7 (*The Message Translation*)

"No man can serve two masters... ye cannot serve God and mammon."

Matthew 6:24

Loyalty is faithfulness, devotion to a person, a vision, cause or a place. It is total and absolute allegiance to a man, in this case, your Pastor.

Loyalty exists because of authority. There are powers and authorities that control life, one of such, is the authority of pastors. You must be loyal to them, submit to their authority so you can enjoy the anointing and grace upon their lives. Remember only what you recognize and respect works for you.

Biblical loyalty is not slavery; it is a basic principle of life that is worth practicing in the church and the world at large. That some church leaders and Christians make mistakes is not an excuse to be disloyal to them thereby violating godly principles. We should uphold godly principles and practice them as God instructs. Loyalty, therefore, is a virtue that must be cultivated. It shows singleness of followership and purpose.

Duality means you are not loyal. None can have and serve two masters equally; he will definitely prefer one to the other. In a nutshell, one will be LOVED and the other USED.

"Ten thousand people may teach you about Christ, but I am your only father..."

1 Corinthians 4:15(*CEV*)

Here are some self-examination questions of loyalty:

- Can you pass the test of loyalty?

- Are you faithful?

- Can you be trusted?

- Faithfulness is required in loyalty.

"...It is required in stewards, that a man be found faithful."

1 Corinthians 4:2

A loyal and faithful person is an asset to a man of God and to the world at large. In proving one's loyalty, the following tests are necessary:

1. The test of fire

2. The test of distance

3. The test of time

Most people are loyal in an ideal situation, but easily become disloyal when under pressure. We read about the three Hebrew boys, Shedrach, Mishach, and Abednego, who remained faithful to their faith in God even in the heart of the fiery furnace. When your loyalty and faithfulness go through the test of fire, will it stand?

Again, some tend to be loyal when their object of loyalty is around; that is eye- service, and it fades away with time. Time will definitely reveal pretenders. Therefore, leadership should be wary of trusting people easily. To trust people easily without them going through these tests is a sign of weakness on the part of leadership.

3. The Protocol of Honour

"Let the elders that rule well be counted worthy of double HONOUR, especially they who labour in the word and doctrine."

1 Timothy 5:17

"...to know them which labour among you, and are over you in the Lord, and admonish you; and to esteem them very highly in love for their work's sake..."

1 Thessalonians 5:12

Honour is respect and esteem towards God and higher authorities over you. Honour is respect accorded to your Pastor.

Wise children must discover and engage in this protocol for their spiritual fathers to open up their heart of hearts and pour blessings on them. Men of

God have many hearts, and honour is one of the protocols that can open up the one that harbors *the blessing*. When you provoke a man of God positively, through an art of venison, he'll definitely impart your life fully. There are superior graces; the grace you don't respect and sow into won't bless you.

Honour is one of the principal keys that determine the operations of God; there is no way you can experience a victorious Christian life without this protocol.

The way to a man's heart is through HONOUR and respect, no longer through food and sex as earlier believed. Practical honour is more important than love, skills, abilities etc.

"A Son honoureth his father and a servant his master: if then I be a father, where is mine HONOUR? And if I be a master, where is my fear?"

Malachi 1:6

"...and no man taketh this HONOUR unto himself, but he that is called of God, as was Aaron."

Hebrews 5:4

Honour is the secret passage to the throne of God. It is what determines your place in destiny. Therefore, identify and celebrate grace, especially superior ones. Honour your spiritual father every step of the way. Avoid every act of dishonor. In the process of serving a pastor, develop divine instinct; it's not everything that you will receive instructions for. You may need to use your initiative sometimes. *Remember, nature is not always fair, if you break any law of nature, you pay for it.* A rebellious life has no future. An act of dishonor can open the door for the enemy to enter and build a stronghold in someone's life. Curses are conceived in the womb of dishonor.

"Remember them which have the rule over you, who have

spoken unto you the word of God: whose faith follow, considering the end of their conversation."

Hebrews 13:7

A Minister and a Ministry you do not receive and support cannot answer to your life's need. Understand the dynamics of relating with your pastors and leaders through the appropriate channels. Be responsive to their needs as much as you can. *Remember, we may be equal before God as human beings but in status and responsibilities, we differ.*

#4. The Protocol of Love and Service

"Look not every man on his own things, but every man also on the things of others."

Philippians 2: 4

"Let no man seek his own, but every man another's wealth."

1 Corinthians 10:24

"With good will doing service, as to the Lord, and not to man: knowing that whatsoever good thing any man doeth, the same shall be receive of the Lord..."

Ephesians 6:7-8

True followers of Christ must have to identify their true ministry and live for it. Pattern your service philosophy after that of Christ. Satisfy your conscience by giving your best as God gave you His best. Service is worshipping God, rendering service to Him and humanity. Truly, service at its best is worship, and worship at its best is living sacrifice. We are called to serve God and His servants set over our lives as pastors and leaders. You cannot serve God without serving people. *There is hierarchy in the Kingdom of God before service will get to God it must first meet people's needs.*

Your commitment to God hinges on your commitment to the person set above you.

Commitment and love are both functions of service and they are inseparable. You do it for the Lord as you follow and serve those He set above you. You can't serve God without serving them. Commitment and love motivates service. Genuine service to God and your Pastor encompasses your time, finances, possession, praises, worship, selflessness, integrity, sacrifice etc.

When you touch God's heart with your service and worship, He will see to it that you lack no good thing. Your sacrificial service of today will pays for your errors of tomorrow. Therefore, serve because your life depends on it.

Service is a vital tool for greatness and struggle-free life. Render gainful services in the Lord's vineyard, always watch out for service protocols and instinct. Endear yourself to the heart of your pastor through your service. Let him have the testimony of your service as Apostle Paul had of Timothy in the following scriptures:

"For I have no man likeminded, who will naturally care for your state for all seek their own, not the things which are Jesus Christ's. But ye know the proof of him, that, as a son with the father, he hath served with me in the gospel."

Philippians 2:20 - 22

"Receive him therefore in the Lord with all gladness; and hold such in reputation: Because for the work of Christ he was nigh unto death, not regarding his life, to supply your lack of service toward me."

Philippians 2:29 - 30

".... take mark, and bring him with thee for he is profitable to me for the ministry."

2 Timothy 4:11

The above are testimonies of service rendered to Apostle Paul and the church of God. There are many more of such testimonies recorded all through the scripture especially in the epistles.

Strive to make your pastor and leaders in the House of God have a beautiful and inspiring testimony of you.

Every great Minister and Ministry should have such testimonies. Service is a responsibility and responsibility is a divine order. No one can really be great in the Kingdom without passing the examination of service. You serve to go up, you serve to lead, the best way to go up is down; that's service way!

Absolute loyalty, love, humility, faithfulness and commitment are all necessary ingredients of service. God's service is not something you pick up from a weekend conference. You must commit your life to it. Service gives honour and favour, serve and be served!

If you don't allow the Bible to teach you the things you need to know, then life will teach you with its harsh reality.

CHAPTER FOUR

THE CONCEPT OF THE PROPHET'S REWARD

"A prophet is not without honour, but in his own country, and among his own kin, and in his own house."

Mark 6: 4

CHAPTER # 4

THE CONCEPT OF THE PROPHET'S REWARD

"He that receiveth you receiveth me, and he that receiveth me receiveth him that sent me. He that receiveth a prophet in the name of a prophet shall receive a prophet's REWARD; and he that receiveth a righteous man in the name of righteous man shall receive a righteous man's reward. And whosoever shall give to drink unto one of those little ones a cup of cold water only in the name of a disciple, verily I say unto you, he shall in no wise lose his reward."

Mathew 10:40 – 42

The ministry of caring for the Pastors, Prophets, Apostles, Evangelist, Teachers etc who are workers in God's vineyard is indeed a glorious one. When we engage ourselves in this regard, we enjoy the lifetime reward that comes through it.

There are various blessings which God designs for the benefit of his people, but not everyone in His vineyard gets them. The variation is on how individuals position themselves to understand how these blessings come.

The primary channel for such blessings is your relationship with the man of God set over you. This is God's design; therefore, you need to maintain a pleasant relationship with your pastor all the way. When you allow God to use you for the man of God, God will also use him for you in return.

What you make happen for the man of God, God will make happen for you.

Your Pastor is God's anointed servant and messenger sent to be a blessing to you; he's your spiritual father!

THE PROPHET'S REWARD

"The one who plants is just as important as the one who waters and each one will be paid for what they do."

1 Corinthians 3:8 (*CEV*)

You can receive a prophet's reward when you: receive and embrace a prophet in the name of a prophet. You can also get it by supporting a prophet through your givings to him and his ministry.

Receiving a prophet because he is a servant of God notwithstanding his age, humanity, background, race, flaws will earn you this reward. Receiving him is receiving Christ, and receiving Christ is receiving God. Therefore, whatever you do to your pastor you do unto God Who placed him over your life.

You must understand that your Pastor is either for your rising or for your falling. If you receive and embrace his ministry then you are set for a rising, the reverse is also true if you treat him with disdain. Position yourself as an arrow in his quiver, God launches people into their destinies by using mighty men and your pastor is one of such men. How well your pastor launches you is a function of your relationship with him. He can launch you into your destiny and greatness or throw you into the bush.

What really is the Prophet's Reward?

The prophet's reward is simply the reward you get based on your understanding of who your prophet is and how you care for him. If you welcome and receive a prophet as one who speaks and works for God, you will receive the same reward as the prophet. In other words, you are entitled to the same reward as the prophet when you receive a prophet in his capacity as a prophet. What a privilege! What a glorious blessing! This is truly awesome!

From the scripture, we learnt that receiving a prophet, a righteous man and giving a cup of water to a disciple, are all the same thing with the same purpose. When you receive a prophet because he is a prophet not minding his humanity, status, weakness, etc you'll have a reward.

When you dishonor a righteous man probably because of too many fake prophets, and you fail to have regard for the genuine ones; you'll lose your reward.

When you honour someone because he is a disciple of Christ, indisputably, you must have your reward. Remember a prophet is both a righteous man and a disciple; as such your reward will be both earthly and eternal.

Let's consider some instances in the Bible where people received the prophets and the results they got...

#1. The Widow of Zarephath (*1 Kings 17: 9-24*)

"...*fetch me, I pray thee, a little water in a vessel, that I may drink....bring me, I pray thee, a morsel of bread in thine hand...fear not; go and do as thou hast said: but make me there of a little cake first, and bring it unto me and after make for thee and for they son...the barrel of meal shall not waste, neither shall the cruse of oil fail, until the day that the Lord sendeth rain upon the earth."*

1 Kings 17:10-14

Here is a beautiful encounter between Prophet Elijah and the Widow of Zarephath. Though she wasn't quite sensitive to key into this life-time opportunity the first time, but God in His grace proved Himself faithful in her life.

Sometimes and many times too, the man of God can encourage you to give in order to provoke a blessing upon yourself. He doesn't do it because he's in need, but so your destiny account will be credited, especially if he noticed lack of sensitivity to the move of the Holy Spirit on your part.

Remember, the prophet brought the blessing to the

woman in her home. You don't have to be very buoyant to give. What was little in her eyes fed the family and the prophet throughout the drought period. She also had the miracle of having her dead son restored back to life.

Whenever you have a little that can't be released, then, you have a little that can't be multiplied.

#2. The Shunamite Woman (*2 Kings 4:8-37*)

"...and it fell on a day, that Elisha passed to Shunem, where was a great woman; and she constrained him to eat bread. And so it was as oft as he passed by, he turned in thither to eat bread...and she said unto her husband, behold now, I perceive that this is an holy man of God, which passeth by us continually .Let us make a little chambers; I pray thee, on the walls and let us set for him there a bed, and a table, and a stool and a candle stick: and it shall be, when he cometh to us, that he shall turn in thither."

2 Kings 4:8-10

This is the story of a very powerful, intelligent, and influential house wife. She was able and quick to perceive the anointing upon a man of God. She perceived that a particular man that always passes by was not an ordinary person, he's an extraordinary person. He may be poor and looks tattered physically, but there's more about him. So she keyed into his anointing, and ensured life became comfortable for the prophet. She provided food, shelter and even library- a reading table for him. Anointing flows better under a comfortable zone. Your pastor may not have time for you if he's fending for himself.

Whatever that woman did for the prophet was without an ulterior motive, as she didn't even know then that the prophet was capable of giving her a miracle son.

If you attach too much importance to your giving, you

may not get the best from it. Remember the prophet's reward comes from God not from the pastor.

You don't give to the prophets because they have need or that they are starving, rather it is an art of covenant practice on your part. God is able to make all grace abound in your life.

You don't give to prophets to make them subservient to you or so that you can manipulate them to suit your desires, but you subscribe into the anointing to get the blessing of the anointing when you welcome them with open arms.

Importantly, you must note that the Shunamite woman did everything with the approval and support of her husband. Women should learn to seek for their husband's approval when rendering support to a prophet to avoid any form of suspicion.

#3. The Philippians Generosity

"Not withstanding ye have done well , that you did communicate with my affliction..

..... that in the beginning of the gospel, when I departed from Macedonia, no church communicate with me as concerning giving and receiving, but ye only.

For even in Thessalonica, ye sent once and again into my necessity. Not because I desire a gift: but I desire fruit that may abound to your account... I am full, having received of Epaphroditus the things which were sent from you, an odour of a sweet smell, a sacrifice acceptable, well pleasing to God.

But my God shall supply all your need according to his riches in glory by Christ Jesus. "

Philippians 4:14-19

The Christians in Philippi graciously helped Apostle Paul. They were taught the same things like the other churches, but by instinct, they understood the importance of giving to a travelling man of God.

Most pastors are shy to mention giving, prophet offering or sacrificial giving to their congregations, maybe because they don't want to sound greedy or overbearing.

Always discern the financial need of your pastor anywhere you find yourself and do something about it. Take for instance, what do you gain by having two or three mobile devices when your pastor has none? Same goes for cars and other enhancing amenities. It's really to your detriment because as your spiritual father, he ought to be comfortable in order to minister to you and intercede for you. Relate to him truly as your father, meet his needs as much as you have the ability and he will willingly and happily increase your capacity of giving through prayers.

Apostle Paul said, "*My God shall supply all your needs*" this is a prophetic declaration from his heart of hearts. Most people do not know what this scripture means. This is purely a blessing from your prophet. Having tasted of your venison like Isaac, he releases the blessings on you without holding back. There is no power on earth that can hinder such decrees from coming to fulfillment.

Though we understand that the prophet's reward comes from God, yet your pastor imparts grace upon you, which in turn hastens your blessing by providing a short- cut: grace is a short-cut to your miracles.

#4. A Woman with an Alabaster Jar

"... there came a woman having an alabaster box of ointment of spikenard very precious; and she broke the box, and poured it on his head."

Mark 14:3

"...she is come aforehand to anoint my body to the burying."

Mark 14:8

"...wheresoever this gospel shall be preached throughout the whole world, this also that she hath done shall be spoken of for a memorial of her."

Mark 14:9

In Bethany, at the house of Simon the leper, Mary the sister of Martha and Lazarus, anointed Jesus Christ with a very costly perfume. She was indirectly preparing the body of Christ for burial. This incident was remarkable as far as Christ was concerned because it was just a few days before his crucifixion.

How did she gain insight into the death and burial of Christ? Remember, even the disciples were yet to ascertain the fact about Christ's crucifixion then. How in the world did she understand this mystery that was hid for ages? Christ said:

"...unto you it is given to know the mystery of the kingdom of God. But unto them that are without, all things are done in parables."

Mark 4: 11

"...for the children of this world are in their generation wiser than the children of light"

Luke 16: 8

Jesus said to the disciples that this act of faith and love demonstrated by Mary would be heard world over as a memorial to her credit. *A supernatural breakthrough requires the sowing of a significant seed.*

"Whatsoever things are true, whatsoever things are honest, whatsoever things are just, whatsoever things are pure, whatsoever things are lovely, whatsoever things are of good report; if there be any praise, think on these things."

Philippians 4: 8

CHAPTER FIVE

THE DYNAMICS OF GIVING

"Share every good thing you have with anyone who teaches you what God has said."

Galatians 6:6 (*CEV*)

"Let him that is taught in the word communicate unto him that teacheth in ALL good things."

Galatians 6:6

CHAPTER # 5

THE DYNAMICS OF GIVING

"The husbandman that laboureth must be first partaker of the fruits"

2 Timothy 2:6

"Church leaders who do their job well deserve to be paid twice as much, especially if they work hard at preaching and teaching... workers are worth their pay."

1 Timothy 5:17-18 (CEV)

"Let the elders that rule well be counted worthy of DOUBLE HONOUR, especially they who labour in the word and Doctrine...the labourer is worthy of his reward."

1 Timothy 5:17-18

A worker deserves payment more so when he is a prophet. He should receive double payment of financial rewards and honour. Honour here has to do with respect, loyalty, submission etc. As we have said above, he should receive all these plus financial remuneration. He is a worker that should be adequately taken care of by his employer: God and members of the Church- this is another aspect of the Double Payment.

"If we have sown unto you spiritual things, is it a great thing if we shall reap your carnal things?"

1 Corinthians 9:11

Apostle Paul sounded beggarly in the scripture above because the Christians in Corinth were foolish, insensitive and ignorant. They were giving to other ministers who were not directly involved with their salvation testimony instead of their spiritual father, Apostle Paul.

Most Christians are like them today, they give to great, senior and popular ministers while their Spiritual fathers are in want. They do not know what they stand to gain by caring for their pastors.

Who is your SPIRITUAL FATHER?

The following points give us clearer picture of the attributes of your spiritual father:

- Your spiritual father is your pastor.

- He's God servant in charge of the church where you worship.

- He is the Pastor, an Apostle, a Teacher, an Evangelist or a Prophet in charge of that local Assembly where you worship.

- He may be the President/ Founder/ General Overseer of the church.

- He may also be the ordained pastor sent to serve as God's Servant in charge of the church where you worship.

This book is not saying that we should not give to other ministers, but that emphasis or priorities should be on our local Assembly Pastors who directly breastfeed us daily. God traces and identifies a Christian through his local church. If your ministry has branches worldwide, then you have two Spiritual fathers – the General Overseer and the Resident Pastor of your local church in case you do not worship at the Headquarters.

FINANCIAL OBLIGATIONS TO PASTORS

Giving to Prophets is a necessary obligation for believers. It is the responsibility of Christians to support their spiritual fathers financially. Christians must be extravagant in their act of benevolence to their Pastors.

"Let him that is taught in the word communicate unto him that teacheth in all good things."

Galatians 6:6

"... for the workman is worthy if his meat."

Mathew 10:10

The responsibilities of a local church pastor to

members are enormous. This includes teaching, preaching, counseling, prayers, impartation, caring, hospitality, intercession, mentoring, etc, on a daily basis. The members should also render their due obligations to their Pastors. These responsibilities primarily have to do with but not limited to financial support. It is the right of a pastor to benefit financially and otherwise from members of his congregation here on earth. This is as a way of communicating back to him.

However, many Christians do not do this. Pastor needs your money, your encouragement, your compassion, your prayers, your kindness, your company, your partnership, your phone call etc. All these you can give to him with interest to encourage him in the good work that the Lord called him to do.

In the Bible, the different kinds of offerings taught

include:

- Tithe offering

- Prophet offering

- Worship offering

- Sacrificial offering

- Building/project offering

- Welfare offering

- First fruit offering

- Widow's mite

- Seed faith

- Vow Offering

"My people are ruined because they don't know what's right or true."

Hosea 4:6 (Message)

Knowledge is vital to your placement in life and destiny. Engage yourself in acquiring relevant and updated information to be a master in life. *"An ignorant child of God suffers same fate with sinners."*

An improved knowledge on the different kinds of offerings listed above will enhance our walk with the Lord and produce more blessings for us.

Tithe Offering:

This is a fundamental obligation and principle of the kingdom. It is a covenant mystery for kingdom practitioners. Tithe is the tenth part of your income. Personally, I believe that paying a tenth part is even for beginners, one can pay as much as twenty – fifty percent (20-50%) of his earnings as tithe in demonstration of his love and faith towards God. For six years now, I have been paying 20% of my earning as tithe and the enormous blessings are evident in my life and family.

"Tithe, like every other giving, is not a donation but a spiritual transaction designed to provoke heaven. Every

other giving will give you returns but only tithe gives security."

Bishop David Oyedepo

Remember, "whatever 90% cannot do in your life 100% can't do it!"

"Bring ye all the tithe into the storehouse, that there may be meat in mine house, and prove me now herewith, saith the Lord of host, if I will not open you the windows of heaven and pour you out a blessing, that there shall not be room enough to receive it. "

Malachi 3:10

Always be excited to present your tithe to God for it honours Him and puts Him first in your order of priorities. If it's possible pay your tithes with clean and mint currency notes not the rumpled or dirty ones. Remember your tithe honours God's position in your life. Don't eat your tithe, it's like deliberately eating poison. When you don't pay your tithe, your life becomes tight!

Prophet Offering:

"If we have sown in to you spiritual things, is it a great thing if we shall reap your carnal things?"

1 Corinthians 9: 11

"Who goeth a warfare any time at his own charges? Who planteth a vineyard and eateth not of the fruit thereof? Or who feedeth a flock, and eateth not of the milk of the flock?"

1 Corinthians 9:7

"Let him that is taught in the word communicate unto him that teacheth in all good things."

Galatians 6: 6

"Don't you know that people who work in the temple make their living from what is brought to the temple? Don't you know that a person who serves at the altar is given part of what is offered? In the same way, the lord wants everyone who preaches the good news to make a living from preaching this message."

1 Corinthians 9:14 (*CEV*)

"The husbandman that laboureth must be the first partaker of the fruits"

2 Timothy 2:6

Prophet offering is an offering presented honourably to pastors to encourage, appreciate and support them in the work they have been called to do.

It is a way of communicating- sharing material blessings and benefits with them. Present it honourably, if it is financial, you can put it in an envelope. Understand that no amount is too much or too small, to give to a prophet provided the motive is genuine and the heart is right.

Recall the mystery of the venison as found in **Genesis 27: 1 - 46**; a father blesses a child when his stomach is full and his heart is merry. If you allow him to bless you with an empty and hungry stomach, the result may not be good enough.

Worship Offering:

"One gives freely, yet grows all the richer; another withholds what he should give, and only suffers want"

Proverbs 11:24 (*ESV*)

"You people are robbing me, your God. And here you are ,asking, "how are we robbing you?" You are robbing me of the offerings and of ten percent that belongs to me."

Malachi 3:8 (*CEV*)

"...he which soweth sparingly shall reap also sparingly; and he which soweth bountifully shall reap also bountifully."

2 Corinthians 9:6

Another name for worship offering is freewill or general offering. It is an amount of money given to God in appreciation for His provision and sustenance. The purpose is to support the work of the ministry. Offerings should honour God and prove your passion for Him; this is why it's an act of worship. You should not give a ridiculous amount from your earning as offering as most ignorant people do. God places value on your offering just like in tithe. It is ridiculous to pay a tithe of two thousand dollars ($2000) and give an offering of fifty or hundred dollars. You should ensure you give your offering in mint just as in tithe. "The quality of your offering determines the quantity of your blessing or harvest".

Sacrificial Offering:

"For to their power, I bear record, yea, and beyond their power they were willing of themselves."

2 Corinthians 8:3

"They that sow in tears shall reap in joy. He that goeth forth and weepeth, bearing precious seed, shall doubtless come again with rejoicing, bringing his sheaves with him."

Psalm 126:5-6

"Therefore doth my father love me, because I lay down my life, that I might take it again?"

John 10: 17

Sacrifice is giving up something of value for something else considered more important. Life generally is sacrificial. Sacrifice moves the heart of God in our direction.

Sacrifice is giving something that costs you much to God because you're trusting him for a visitation. The altar of Sacrifice is where curses are broken and where God swears a blessing upon His people. A Sacrifice is defined by the cost it places on the individual not by its volume. Serving and giving to a pastor is sacrificial. You can sacrificially pay your Spiritual father monthly salary, pay the School fees of his children, or sponsor church programmes. You can devote your life, resources, knowledge to promoting God's work. Like the Reverend Fathers and Sisters, you can devote your life to God as living sacrifice to serve Him in His vineyard all your life.

If this kingdom does not cost you, this kingdom will not pay you.

Building/ Project Offering:

"…and they brought the lord's offering to the work of the tabernacle of the congregation and for all his service, and for the holy garments."

Exodus 35: 21

"…so David bought the threshing floor and the oxen for fifty shekel of silver."

2 Samuel 24: 24

"…that he was worthy for whom he should do this: for he loveth our nation, and he hath built us a synagogue."
Luke 7: 4-5

This is another type of sacrificial offering. You give towards the church projects. Paying church rent, acquiring plots of land for church building, sponsoring church programs etc are part of the project offering.

Welfare Offering:

"If a brother or sister be naked, and destitute of daily food...not withstanding ye give them not those things which are needful for the body; what doth it profit?"

James 2:15 - 16

"He that giveth into the poor shall not lack; but he that hideth his eyes shall have many a curse."

Proverbs 28:27

"Take care of God's needy people and welcome strangers unto your home."

Romans 12: 13 (*CEV*)

Welfare offering is also charity offering. It is an offering given to the needy in God's vineyard. They could be the missionaries, widows, orphans etc. It's hospitality in nature.

First Fruit Offering:

"...ye shall also give unto the priest the first of your

dough, that he may cause the blessing to rest in thine house."

Ezekiel 44:30

First fruit offering is the offering of the first part of your harvest, increase or profit. First fruit is a mystery most Christians don't practice because they don't understand it. The first fruit principle is important because it opens the womb of life and the womb of the year. Anything you pay first fruit on becomes holy, sanctified and secured forever. *You pay your First fruit to your Pastor.*

The Widow's Mite:

"Everyone else gave what they didn't need, but she is very poor and gave everything she had."

Luke 21:4 (*CEV*)

"Although they were going through hard times and were very poor, they were glad to give generously. They gave as much as they could afford and even more, simply because they wanted to."

2 Corinthians 8: 2-3 (*CEV*)

The Widow's mite is giving your all. It's a higher degree of sacrificial giving with absolute trust and reliance on God for His sustenance and divine provisions.

Challenged and poor Christians do not have any excuse not to give because everyone has something to give, no matter how little. They can give away their challenges and poverty through this form of giving done with an act of faith. The widow of Zarephath is an example in this regard.

"Even the widow needs to give for her window to be opened."

The following explain the Widow's Mite offering clearer:

- Giving your transport fare and trekking home from service

- Giving your only car, phone, television, laptop, and do without them until you get another one

- Giving things you place so much value on for the Gospel, they should be important and valuable to you not things you have no regards for anymore.

- Allowing your only child to become a reverend father or sister can also be viewed as a widow's mite.

Seed Faith:

"Cast thy bread upon thy waters: for thou shall find it after many days."

Ecclesiastes 11:1

"…he which soweth sparingly shall reap also sparingly; and he which soweth bountifully shall reap also bountifully."

2 Corinthians 9:6

Seed faith is something sown for future reward. It usually comes with interest. Every seed you sow into the kingdom has a way of coming back to you with multiplied harvest. Seed faith is a covenant mystery that operates the law of seed-time and harvest. Sow great and living seeds today to secure a better future for yourself and loved ones tommorow!

Vow Offering:

"And she vowed a vow, and said, O Lord of hosts, if thou wilt indeed look on the affliction of thine handmaid, and remember me, and not forget thine handmaid, but wilt give unto thine handmaid a man child, then I will give him unto the Lord all the days of his life, and there shall no razor come upon his head."

1 Samuel 1:11

A Vow Offering is a solemn promise binding or committing one to a course of action or a decision earlier made to God. It is your response to God's intervention in your life. Here you take a deliberate decision with a vow of what you will do or give to God after His intervention

Redeem all vows as promptly as possible. This will curb delay which may lead to forgetfulness. God doesn't take pleasure in people who vow and fail to redeem their vows. Take all vows seriously, especially marital vows and vows of celibacy. The decision to be single for the sake of the Gospel is a solemn vow that shouldn't be toyed with. When a person vows to be a priest, he or she shouldn't go back on this vow but should fulfill it!

THE LAW OF CAUSE AND EFFECT

This is also the law of sowing and reaping. Life is built on cause and effect principle. This law returns to you the harvest of whatever you have given or sown. *"Whatever a man sows, that shall he also reap."* *If you cloth a prophet, you automatically cloth your destiny. Sowing into the life of your spiritual father and the ministry is an unending investment for your future.*

There are Christians that decorate their men of God and there are Christians that tear the garment of their men of God like King Saul in the Bible days. Tearing the garment of one's pastor knowingly or unknowingly is equivalent to tearing one's destiny into shreds, be careful!

When you sow a seed, even the earth cannot deny you the harvest. If you sow nothing you reap nothing.

All the types of giving enumerated above affect the prophet in one way or the other.

Whatever financial involvement you engage in the church, it affects the prophet positively. Paying tithe, vows, first fruit, seed faith etc lead to abundance of financial blessing in the storehouse of the church. This as well brings about financial increase and benefits to the man of God. When the man of God's needs are met, there will be free flow of the anointing and he will not struggle to impact and bless members of his congregation.

When members are faithful and committed to their financial obligations and sundries, their prophet is happy, because it's also a sign of his success and improvement.

A seed to God and the man of God is capable of making the pastor happy, encourage him, increase his anointing, raise his hands and keep them up!

No soldier goes to war of life and win the battle by manufacturing the weapons of war on the battleground. Be wise for wisdom is profitable to direct!

CHAPTER SEX

THE OBLIGATION OF PRAYING FOR PASTORS

What a glorious privilege and obligation to pray for our Pastors!

CHAPTER #6

THE OBLIGATION OF PRAYING FOR PASTORS

Prayer is communicating with God. As Christians, we should learn to pray without ceasing, pray in and out of season. We are to pray all manner of prayers, prayer of intercession, prayer of agreement, prayer of faith etc, and our hearts should always be in our prayers for it to work.

"I exhort, therefore, that, first of all, supplications, prayers, intercessions, and giving of thanks, be made for all men...that we may lead a quiet and peaceable life in all godliness and honesty."

1 Timothy 2:1-2

The responsibility of praying for one's pastors is rewarding, both to the pastors as well as to the members, because the labourer is the first partaker of the harvest. We should pray for our pastor so they won't succumb to temptations and challenges. They also need our prayers to stay away from wicked and unreasonable men.

Our Lord Jesus Christ, the King of kings showed us an example that leaders as well need our prayers. He invited some of His beloved and trusted disciples to pray with Him shortly before His arrest. Our men of God and leaders are not too anointed or too old to need our prayers too!

"...He said to them, "I am so sad that I feel as if I am dying. Stay here and keep awake with me." He came back and found his disciples sleeping, so He said to Peter, "can't any of you stay awake with me for just one hour...you want to do what is right but you are weak"

Mathew 26:38 - 41 (*CEV*)

Many times, we think pastors do not need prayers because by their calling, they are supposed to keep watch and pray all the time. Yet, we should pray for them because the challenge of the office can be overwhelming sometimes.

The protocol of prayer for pastors is one of the strategies we can employ to receive the pastor's reward.

Behind every successful pastor and a great ministry are members who are willing to sacrifice their time in prayers for their pastors.

Satan always targets pastors to attack them and disrupt the work of the ministry; this is why our daily prayers for them are necessary. We should faithfully engage in all forms of prayers for them as well as other saints of God in the vineyard.

TYPES OF PRAYER

"Praying always with all prayer and supplication in the spirit, and watching thereunto with all perseverance and supplication for all saints."

Ephesians 6:18

Prayer of Supplications: This is also the prayer of petition. It means to ask or entreat God for something. When fueled by zeal, it becomes an attitude.

Prayer of Intercession: This is pleading on behalf of someone else. It is the heart of prayer for pastors, saints and churches generally. Any Christian who is matured in the things of God will engage in this type of prayer. It takes the attention off you and places it on others. Praying only for oneself amounts to selfishness and immaturity.

"...pray for us, that the word of the lord may have free course, and be glorified, even as it is with you: and that we may be delivered from unreasonable and wicked men: for all men have not faith."

2 Thessalonians 3:1-2

"Withal praying also for us, that God would open unto us a door of utterance, to speak the mystery of Christ, for which I am also in bonds."

Colossians 4:3

"And for me, that utterance may be given unto me, that I may open my mouth boldly, to make known the mystery of the gospel."

Ephesians 6:19

"Pray for us: for we trust we have a good conscience, in all things willing to live honestly. "

Hebrews 13: 18

Prayer of Thanksgiving: Our prayer for pastors and saints of God must include thanksgiving. This should not be missing in our prayer times. We thank God for the lives of those sent to lead us; we show our love and respect for them by continually thanking God for their lives. A sincere heart of thanksgiving must have honour, which is the combination of praise and worship.

Prayer of thanksgiving shows faith in God, and it hastens God's intervention in our lives.

"Continue in prayer, and watch in the same with thanksgiving."

Colossians 4: 2

TEN MAJOR REASONS WHY WE SHOULD PRAY
FOR OUR PASTORS

- It's our responsibility to pray for them.

- We are blessed when we do it for *"the labourer is the first partaker of the fruits."*

- They pray for us too.

- They are our spiritual fathers.

- Praying for them helps in promoting the work of the kingdom.

- It demonstrates our submission, love, honour and loyalty to their authority.

- They asked us to pray for them, *"Brethren, pray for us"* (1 Thessalonians 5:25).

- Christ admonished us to do so in His law; *"Bear ye one another's burdens, and so fulfill the law of Christ"*. (*Galatians 6:2*).

As we pray for them, their Ministry will have its expression in our lives.

- We pray for them because wise children pray for their fathers.

As we pray for our Men of God, we should focus on the following areas:

i) Utterance: that they may receive utterance from the Holy Spirit (*Ephesians 6:19*)

ii) Protection: they need protection from wicked and unreasonable men (*2 Thessalonians 3:2*)

iii) Strength: that God's strength will be made perfect in their weakness (*2 Corinthians 12:9*)

iv)   Obedience to God's word and instruction
      (*2 Corinthians 10:5*)

v)   Right attitude in ministry

vi)   Constant spiritual refreshment

vii) Financial blessing

viii) Open doors and connections

ix)   Miracles, signs and wonders

x)   Grace and supernatural favour

xi)   Knowledge, wisdom, revelation and
      intelligence

xii) Fruit and gifts of the Holy Spirit

xiii) Empowerment by the Holy Spirit

xiv) Pray, for all that's required for successful
      ministry and life.

xv)   Emotional intelligence

xvi) Accountability

Take the responsibility of prayers seriously in Churches. No enemy can gain access into a fervent praying church.

Prayer brings solution to all challenges, especially on matters properly addressed and handed over to God. A praying church is an active, vibrant and result oriented one. Conversely, the dearth of prayers in a church gives room for Satan to manifest by bringing in struggle and failures. Check yourself sincerely and know if you are engaging in this act effectively.

"A small decision now can change all your tomorrows."
Robert Schuller.

CHAPTER SEVEN

GENERAL OBLIGATIONS TO PASTORS

"Finally, brethren, whatsoever things are true, whatsoever things are honest, whatsoever things are pure, whatsoever things are lovely, whatsoever things are of good report; if there be any virtue, and if there be any praise, THINK ON THESE THINGS."

Philippians 4:8

CHAPTER 7

GENERAL OBLIGATIONS TO PASTORS

There are responsibilities we should have towards our pastors. These responsibilities range from Christian ethics to etiquette and protocol.

Though these responsibilities sound so infinitesimal and insignificant, yet they are very necessary towards having a good working and gainful relationship with our pastors.

"Therefore to him that knoweth to do good, and doeth it not, to him it is a SIN."

James 4: 17

"Prove all things; hold fast that which is good."

1 Thess. 5:21

1) Always appreciate your pastor. *"Overwhelm them with appreciation.* **1 Thessalonians 5:12** (The Message).

Our pastors have charge over us so we should appreciate them.

Ingratitude means you don't love and believe in them; a pastor you don't believe in cannot bless you.

2) Be submissive *"...and submit yourselves: for they watch for your souls, as they that must give account, that they may do it with joy, and not with grief: for that is unprofitable for you"*. (*Hebrews 13:17*).

3) Be loyal to them. *"Ten thousand people may teach you about Christ, but I am your only father."* (*1 Corinthians 4:15*)

4) Always esteem your pastor. *"...and to esteem them very highly in love for their work's sake...and be at peace among your selves."* (*1 Thessalonians 5:13*)

5) Honour them at all times. *"Let the elders that rule well be counted worthy of double honour, especially they who labour in the word and doctrine".(1 Timothy 5:17)*

6) Always pray for them. *"Pray for us: for we trust we have a good conscience, in all things willing to live honestly"* (*Hebrews 13:18*). Pray for them continually.

7) Support them financially. *"Let him that is taught in the word communicate unto him that teacheth in all good things"* (*Galatians 6:6*). Make provision for his needs. Discern his heart cry.

8) Respect and obey them all the time. *"Obey them that have the rule over you..."*(*Hebrews 13.17*). Respect him for the grace he carries.

9) Love your spiritual father. *"And to esteem them very highly in love for their work's sake and*

be at peace among yourselves." *(1 Thessalonians 5:13).*

10)Remember them always. *"Remember them which have the rule over you, who have spoken unto you the word of God: whose faith followeth, considering the end of their conversation."* *(Hebrews 13:7).*

To remember is to be mindful, thoughtful and to keep in mind. You must be mindful of your pastor at all times. Be his champion and son of consolation.

11)You must follow his examples. *"For yourselves know how ye ought to follow us: for we behaved not ourselves disorderly among you"* (2 Thessalonians 3:7). *"...but followers of them who through faith and patience inherit the promises"* (Hebrews 6: 12).

"...you would be following the example of those who had

faith and were patient until God kept his promise to them"

Hebrews 6:12 (*CEV*)

"Wherefore I beseech you, be ye followers of me."

1 Corinthians 4:16

Other obligations and responsibilities towards our pastors include:

"Our vineyards are in blossom; we must catch the little foxes that destroy the vineyards"

Songs of Solomon 2:15 (*CEV*)

- Do not judge your pastor for he is not answerable to you.

- Do not gossip about him or with his name, it's very wrong to do so.

- Do not doubt him, it is a sign you do not believe in him. A pastor you do not believe in will not bless you.

- Do not be too familiar with him. Over-familiarity will cost you your miracles. Even if your pastor is your younger brother, your age mate, your in-law, etc, respect the anointing upon his life. When you do this, you are honouring the God that called him.

- Defend him always *"...but they shall speak with the enemies in the gate"* (Psalm 127:5). A well-trained child defends his father at the gate.

- Do not speak against him *"...wherefore then were you not afraid to speak against my servant Moses?"* (Numbers 12:8)

- Love his family, especially his wife.

- Don't throw unnecessary jokes at him.

- Appreciate what gives him joy.

- He shouldn't arrive at any meeting or function before and you shouldn't leave a function or meeting before him, it is disrespectful to do that.

- Let him always lay hands on your head as you kneel down before him. This is a sign of submission and respect for the anointing.

- Don't advertise his weakness and flaws.

- Don't be among those that gang up against their pastors.

- Don't be uncomfortable with his presence.

- Don't be among those who criticize and attack their spiritual parents.

- Don't be a fault finder.

- Do not lie to him.

- Do not show any element of pride and anger before him.

- It's important to say Amen whenever he is preaching or teaching, and be excited by his messages.

- Always take down notes when he is preaching or teaching.

- Don't close your Bible while he is still preaching. It shows disrespect and lack of interest in his preaching.

- Don't be distracted when he is preaching or on the pulpit.

- Don't pitch tents with others against him.

- Always showcase him to other members; take the attention off you to him.

- Do not be a threat to him. Position yourself well and carefully too; don't provoke him to jealousy and selfishness.

- Promote what he promotes.

- Go to him for advice.

- Don't pretend for him to like you, be you and be real.

- Don't destroy other peoples' character because you want him to like you.

- Do not rebel or champion rebellion against him. It is a terrible thing to do. Korah, Dathan & Abiram in the Bible tried it with Moses, but didn't live to tell the story.

- Do not make life and ministry difficult for him; otherwise, your life will become hard too.

- Heap and shower praises on him whenever you are on the pulpit.

"Prove all things; hold fast that which is good."

1 Thessalonians. 5: 21

"Life gives back what you give."

Galatians 6: 7

CHAPTER EIGHT

ROLES AND RESPONSIBILITIES OF PASTORS TO MEMBERS

"…if a man desire the office of a Bishop, he desireth a good work"

1 Timothy 3: 1

CHAPTER #8

ROLES AND RESPONSIBILITIES OF PASTORS TO MEMBERS

"...the Kings of the Gentiles exercise Lordship over them; and they that exercise Authority upon them are called benefactors. But ye shall not be so: but he that is greatest among you, let him be as the younger; and he that is chief, as he that doth serve"

Luke 22:25-26

"I am the good shepherd: the good shepherd giveth his life for the sheep"

John 10:11

"...woe be to the shepherds of Israel that do feed themselves! Should not the shepherds feed the flocks? Ye eat the fat, and ye clothe you with the wool, ye kill them that are fed: but ye feed not the flock"

Ezekiel 34:2-3

"Just as shepherds watch over their sheep, you must watch

over everyone God has PLACED in your care. Do it willingly in order to please God and get your reward, and not simply because you think you must. Let it be something you want to do, instead of something you do merely to make a living. Don't be bossy to those people who are in your care, but set an example for them"

1 Peter 5:2-3 (*CEV*)

We have discussed extensively on the responsibilities of church members to the ministers set over them in this book. God loves orderliness and His instructions are for everyone, both children and parents. We'll look at the responsibilities and roles of pastors to their flocks as we conclude. There is a word for everyone; don't sit on the fence, find out what's said to you and run with it until you've fulfilled them.

Pastors' obligations to members of their congregation are a higher and greater one. It's far beyond the responsibilities of the members towards their spiritual fathers. Pastors have a very serious commitment to God; they are also committed to serving and ministering to God's people.

Therefore, it's important for them to understand the following:

#1. The success of their members is their success and the converse is true as well.

#2. Members are their children and as children, they are bound to err.

#3. The Authority they have is spiritual, different from the type exercised by those in secular jobs. Theirs is to build up and not to destroy the beloved Christians that Jesus Christ paid for their redemption with His blood.

#4. They must understand the power in their spoken words and the authority their tongue wield.

"Take heed therefore unto yourselves, and to all the flock, over the which the Holy ghost hath made you overseers, to

feed the church of God, which he hath purchased with his own blood"

Acts 20:28

"...according to the power which the Lord hath given to edification, and not to destruction"

2 Corinthians 13:10

"But we were gentle among you, even as a NURSE cherisheth her children"

1 Thessalonians 2:7

THE PRIMARY RESPONSIBILITIES OF PASTORS ARE ENUMERATED BELOW:

- They must preach and teach God's word with all passion and zeal. *"But we will give ourselves continually to prayer, and to the Ministry of the World"* (Acts 6:4). *"Simon, son of Jonas, lovest thou me? Feed my sheep"* (John 21:16).

Pastors must take this responsibility very seriously. They must feed their flocks with the truth of God's word, otherwise, they face the risk of losing them to false teachers and to Satan when trials and challenges of life come knocking. They should not hide the truth of any matter the congregation needs to know from them, otherwise, they will be termed deceitful. Pastors should understand that some members know more than the pastors think they know. So, study hard to carry out this function, as members truly appreciate pastors who know the word of God.

- They must be Role models to their flocks. "*Let no man despise thy youth; but be thou an example of the believers, in word, in conversation, in charity, in spirit in faith, in purity*" (*1 Timothy 4:12*).

Remember your life is an epistle. Believers and unbelievers alike are more interested in the activities of a pastor than anyone else.

- They must pray for the members of their congregation. *"...For they watch for your souls..."* (*Hebrews 13:17*).

- They are leaders to the members of their congregation. *"Remember them which have the rule over you, who have spoken unto you the word of God..."* (*Hebrews 13:7*).

God entrusted the responsibility of leading the flocks to Pastors. God will hold them responsible if anything goes wrong with the flock. Pastors must be proactive, bold, smart and knowledgeable in carrying out this responsibility.

- They must comfort and care for the members of their congregation. *"Now we exhort you, brethren, warn them that are unruly, comfort the feeble-minded, support the weak, be patient towards all men"* (*1 Thessalonians 5:14*).

- They must guide and protect them. *"Take heed therefore unto yourselves and to all the flock, over the which the Holy ghost hath made you overseers..."* (Acts 20:28).

It is your duty to guard and guide them against all forms of spiritual and physical assault. Remember, they are a mixed multitude; there are goats and there are sheep. Sheep naturally are very vulnerable and need protection while goats are stronger and stubborn. The pastors should be sensitive to their individual differences and be able to guide aright. In leading them, be selfless and don't show favoritism.

- They must develop, train Leaders and Teachers.

Pastors should endeavour to develop and train teachers and leaders to serve under them. He should trust them enough to handle some matters; this shows maturity. You should allow them time, space and opportunity to grow. Pastors should not do all of the work of the ministry by themselves. Spiritual fathers should also discern the gifts and vision of God for their members and advice them accordingly. *"Remember, children are improved version of their fathers".*

- Pastors should know their members *"I am the Good Shepherd, and know my sheep, and am known of mine"* (*John 10:27*).

- They must Discipline their members.

Pastors should be able to discipline erring and unrepentant members. They should do this without any fear or favour so as to serve as examples to others.

- They must keep clear conscience at all time. *"Pray for us: for we trust we have a good conscience, in all things willing to live honestly"* (*Hebrews 13:18*).

Spiritual fathers should endeavour to keep clear

conscience towards their ministry and members of their congregation always. It might not be easy, but, they need to do this, by loving the members as Christ loves them. Pastors' obligations to members are enormous and cannot be exhaustively discussed in this book. The life manual, the Bible, has the full details of their responsibilities towards the Church.

They should, with the help of the Holy Spirit discharge their roles and responsibilities effectively in order to have a healthy Church and a successful ministry.

Pastors need to realise that recent events and activities of some fake prophets or pastors threaten their office and authority. Therefore, they should always disabuse the minds of their members from such beliefs by working against these deceitful ways. They ought to know that leadership is influence. How many members you are able to win over to your side makes you a good father not how many you are able to destroy or pull down.

Always empower them to stand on their own with the confidence that they can at all times do the right thing.

"Let the elders that rule well be counted worthy of double honour, especially they who labour in the word and doctrine."

1 Timothy 5:17

CHAPTER NINE
GIFT OF PEACE

"For the law of the spirit of life in Christ Jesus hath made me free from the law of sin and death."

Romans 8:2

CHAPTER #9

GIFT OF PEACE

Someone who wants to enjoy serving God must first be born again. Most Christian workers in the church aren't saved, hence they engage in this service with their own human effort instead of drawing strength from the Lord. To anyone who has no relationship with the Creator, service in His vineyard will be endured instead of to be enjoyed.

The relationship with the Almighty God grants one divine access to Him; the Holy Spirit reveals the mind of the Father towards service in His vineyard. The Holy Spirit also reveals to us that the reason why we are saved is to serve and that there is no way you can serve God in His vineyard without serving people especially God's Servant set over you.

The fact that some people are workers in God's house does not make them born again and does not also make them have personal relationship with the Father. *"Working in His vineyard does not influence your relationship with God; it is your relationship that influences your service." Walking with God is not the same as working for God." You can work for God without walking with him, but there is no way you walk with God without working for him.*

Walking with God influences your work for God and not the other way round. Therefore, the relationship with God enables Christians to know that their lives are for service to God and that God calls them according to His divine purpose.

"Whoever claims to live in him must walk as Jesus did"

1 John 2:6 (*NIV*)

Christians should walk and conduct themselves well as Christ did. God rewards every service. There are rewards for everything done in God's vineyard. The reward of eternal and earthly blessings is more valuable than any salary one can think of.

As sanctions are meted out to workers who default in secular jobs, so should it be in God's vineyard. When believers serving as workers in God's vineyard err, they can be sanctioned *for correction* to enable them sit up and perform effectively.

HAVE YOU RECEIVED THE GIFT?

"He asked his disciples, saying, who do men say that I, the son of man, am? They said, "some say John the Baptist, some Elijah, and others Jeremiah or one of the prophets. "

"He said to them, "But who do you say that I am?"Simon Peter answered and said, "You are the Christ, the son of the living God. "

Mathew 16:13-16

This looks very simple, but it's the bedrock of salvation. Salvation begins with knowing Christ in order to have a relationship with Him.

As a Christian worker, do you know Christ or are you merely describing Him with beautiful names, but no relationship with Him? Jesus may be Christ, the Son of the living God to others and to the church where you worship, but Who is He to you personally? He's Christ to your husband, to your wife, to the choir members, to the ushering department, to the youth department, but to you: *Who say ye the son of man* is?

Until you understand and personalize who Christ is, you have no part in Him, you are not connected to Him, so your service is meaningless and your entire life is full of crisis.

Although you are in a church and a worker, yet the devil owns you completely and controls your affairs. When things are not happening favourably for you, you'll think God is unfair. You need to understand that your relationship with God must get through before anything else goes through for you.

HOW DOES ONE KNOW HIM?

"Come now, let us reason together", says the Lord. Though your sins are like scarlet, they shall be as white as snow; though they are red as crimson, they shall be like wool"

Isaiah 1:18 (*NIV*)

"For God so loved the world, that he gave His only begotten Son, that whosoever believeth in him should not perish, but have everlasting life."

John 3:16

"For the wages of sin is death, but the GIFT of God is eternal life through Jesus Christ our Lord."

Romans 6:23

This gift of salvation is special and wonderful. It saves from all manner of condemnation. It is a token from God. Please accept it without procrastination. Jesus Christ is giving you the invitation thus:

"...I stand at the door, and knock, if any man hear my voice, and open the door, I will come in to him, and will sup with him, and he with me."

Revelation 3:20

"... I am the way, the truth and the life: no man cometh unto the father, but by me."

John 14:6

Christ is still knocking at the door of your heart, even now, as you are reading this book. Will you open for Him to come in? Remember, He is the only way for you to salvation – deliverance from sin and its consequence.

"Neither is there salvation in any other, for there is none other name under heaven given among men, whereby we must be saved"

Acts 4:12

As you can see from the above scripture, nothing else gives salvation other than belief in the Name of Jesus and confession that He is Lord of all. Money, political, ethnic or family influence cannot save anyone from sin.

Are you ready to accept him now? If yes, then:

❖ Acknowledge that you are a sinner.

" ...all have sinned and come short of the glory of God."

Romans 3:23

"If we say that we have no sin, we deceive ourselves, and the truth is not in us. If we say that we have not sinned, we make him a liar and his word is not in us."

1 John 1:8-10

"...there is none righteous, no, not one."

Romans 3:10

Put aside your vain garment of religion. Your self-righteousness cannot bring you up to God's standard.

❖ Believe on the Lord

"… believe on the Lord Jesus Christ, and thou shalt be saved, and thy house"

Acts 16:31

"But as many as received him, to them gave he power to become the SONS of God, even to them that BELIEVE on his Name."

John 1:12

❖ Confess your SINS and confess CHRIST as your Lord.

"If we confess our sins, he is faithful and just to forgive us our sins, and to cleanse us from all unrighteousness."

1 John 1:9

"For with the heart man believeth unto righteousness; and with the mouth confession is made unto salvation."

Romans 10:10

Make this declaration:

"Dear Lord God, I thank You for sending Your Son: Jesus Christ to die for me on the Cross of Calvary. I acknowledge Him as the Son of God and the Lord of my life. I accept Him today as my personal Lord and Saviour. Thank You Lord for forgiving and cleansing me of all my sins, in Jesus Name, Amen."

Congratulations! You are now a child of God. Get yourself involved in a good Bible believing Church; be baptized by immersion to fulfill all righteousness as Christ taught us. Do not go back to your sins, live for the Lord henceforth.

"...if any man be in Christ, he is a new creature: old things are passed away, behold, all things are become new"

2 Corinthians 5:17

You are now born again, a new creature in Christ Jesus. You have just started a new life again like a newly born baby. Grow by feeding on God's word and attending Church services regularly. You must at all times keep the fire burning inside you. To do this, have the fear of the Lord within you. Pray always and engage in fasting regularly to build your faith up as well as train you to hear from God.

Your lifestyle henceforth should be that of praise. Live a joyous life, you truly do not lose anything by serving the Lord!

Congratulations once more!

OTHER BOOK BY THE AUTHOR

Other Book By The Author:

THE KING'S MEAT & WINE

...you can enjoy success without compromise!

How can believers succeed in an ungodly environment without tasting the portion of the king's meat and wine? How can they assume their rightful position in an unfriendly environment in which they lack the ability to influence?

As a believer, the ability to thrive successfully in whatever circumstances in life is within you: You have the raw material in you. You are loaded with enormous power to triumph here on earth.

Spencer Dafe Itive in his characteristic style reveals:

❖ How you can avoid the portion of the king's meat and wine.

❖ How to apply the success secrets of Daniel and his companions in an ungodly land like Babylon.

❖ How believers and the church can free themselves from this present entanglement.

Yes, you can really enjoy success without compromise!

ABOUT THE BOOK

How to Receive PASTORS' BLESSINGS...

There are countless blessings in serving God. How to get these blessings remains the fundamental question for Christians who engage in service to God.

Being skillful and talented is not enough. Until certain principles are discovered, understood and sincerely applied, things may not change for the better.

The secret to a world of gainful service in God's kingdom lies in your pastor- God's Servant set over your life. He's your indispensable CHANNEL of God's blessings.

This insightful masterpiece is for those who have genuine hearts of service...

ABOUT THE AUTHOR

SPENCER ITIVE is an anointed Child of God and a teacher of God's word. He's also a role model, Bible scholar, conference speaker, marriage counselor & motivational speaker.

Spencer is married to Agatha Spencer and they have three blessed children: God's Covenant, Rhema and Amen.

www.ingramcontent.com/pod-product-compliance
Lightning Source LLC
LaVergne TN
LVHW041158080426
835511LV00006B/649